KUM◯N®
MATH. READING. SUCCESS.

What is Kumon?

Kumon is the world's largest supplemental education provider and a leader in producing outstanding results. After-school programs in math and reading at Kumon Centers around the globe have been helping children succeed for 50 years.

Kumon Workbooks represent just a fraction of our complete curriculum of preschool-to-college-level material assigned at Kumon Centers under the supervision of trained Kumon Instructors.

The Kumon Method enables each child to progress successfully by practicing material until concepts are mastered and advancing in small, manageable increments. Instructors carefully assign materials and pace advancement according to the strengths and needs of each individual student.

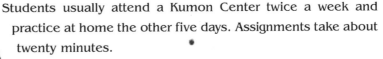

Students usually attend a Kumon Center twice a week and practice at home the other five days. Assignments take about twenty minutes.

Kumon helps students of all ages and abilities master the basics, improve concentration and study habits, and build confidence.

How did Kumon begin?

IT ALL BEGAN IN JAPAN 50 YEARS AGO when a parent and teacher named Toru Kumon found a way to help his son Takeshi do better in school. At the prompting of his wife, he created a series of short assignments that his son could complete successfully in less than 20 minutes a day and that would ultimately make high school math easy. Because each was just a bit more challenging than the last, Takeshi was able to master the skills and gain the confidence to keep advancing.

This unique self-learning method was so successful that Toru's son was able to do calculus by the time he was in the sixth grade. Understanding the value of good reading comprehension, Mr. Kumon then developed a reading program employing the same method. His programs are the basis and inspiration of those offered at Kumon Centers today under the expert guidance of professional Kumon Instructors.

Mr. Toru Kumon
Founder of Kumon

KUMON
MATH. READING. SUCCESS.

What can Kumon do for my child?

Kumon is geared to children of all ages and skill levels. Whether you want to give your child a leg up in his or her schooling, build a strong foundation for future studies or address a possible learning problem, Kumon provides an effective program for developing key learning skills given the strengths and needs of each individual child.

What makes Kumon so different?

Kumon uses neither a classroom model nor a tutoring approach. It's designed to facilitate self-acquisition of the skills and study habits needed to improve academic performance. This empowers children to succeed on their own, giving them a sense of accomplishment that fosters further achievement. Whether for remedial work or enrichment, a child advances according to individual ability and initiative to reach his or her full potential. Kumon is not only effective, but also surprisingly affordable.

What is the role of the Kumon Instructor?

Kumon Instructors regard themselves more as mentors or coaches than teachers in the traditional sense. Their principal role is to provide the direction, support and encouragement that will guide the student to performing at 100% of his or her potential. Along with their rigorous training in the Kumon Method, all Kumon Instructors share a passion for education and an earnest desire to help children succeed.

KUMON FOSTERS:

- A mastery of the basics of reading and math
- Improved concentration and study habits
- Increased self-discipline and self-confidence
- A proficiency in material at every level
- Performance to each student's full potential
- A sense of accomplishment

▶▶ GETTING STARTED IS EASY. Just call us at 877.586.6671 or visit kumon.com to request our free brochure and find a Kumon Center near you. We'll direct you to an Instructor who will be happy to speak with you about how Kumon can address your child's particular needs and arrange a free placement test. There are more than 1,700 Kumon Centers in the U.S. and Canada, and students may enroll at any time throughout the year, even summer. Contact us today.

FIND OUT MORE ABOUT KUMON MATH & READING CENTERS.
Receive a free copy of our parent guide, *Every Child an Achiever,* by visiting
kumon.com/go.survey or calling 877.586.6671

Statue of Liberty

United States of
America

Name Harry

Date 10/38/14

To parents
Have your child trace a path through the maze with his or her finger before using a pencil. Next, have your child use a pencil to complete the maze. When your child is done, give him or her plenty of praise.

■ Draw a line through the maze from the arrow (➡) to the star (★).

1

■ Draw a line through the maze from the arrow (➡) to the star (★).

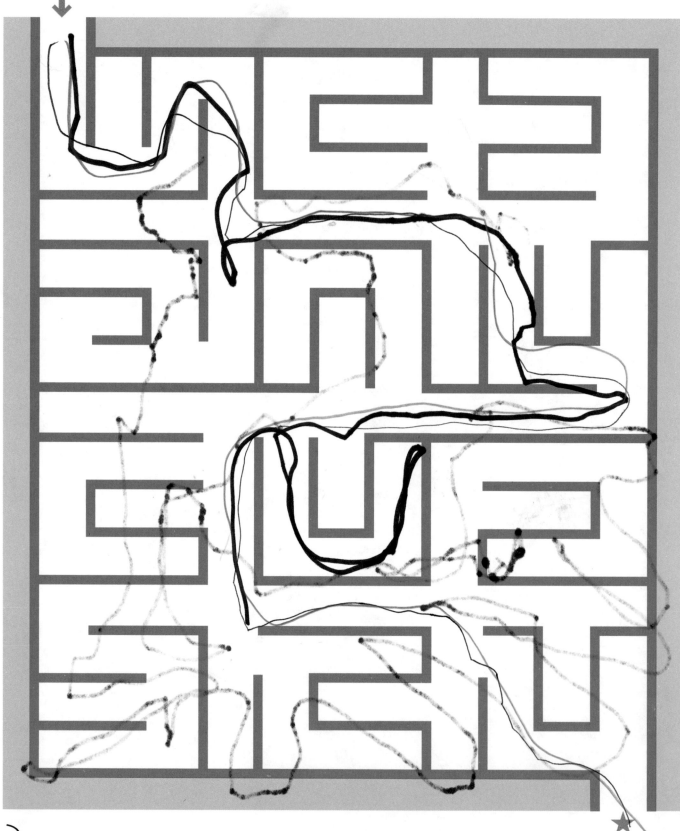

Stonehenge

United Kingdom

To parents
Once your child is finished with this maze, refer to the world map on the last page of this book. There you can show your child where in the world this landmark can be found.

■ Draw a line through the maze from the arrow (➡) to the star (★).

■ Draw a line through the maze from the arrow (➡) to the star (★).

Moai Statues on Easter Island

Chile

To parents

Please help your child understand that the gray areas inside the maze are not obstacles. In other words, the correct path to the exit will take them through some of the gray shaded areas inside the maze.

■ Draw a line through the maze from the arrow (➡) to the star (★).

5

■ Draw a line through the maze from the arrow (➡) to the star (★).

Mount Rushmore

Name

Date

■ Draw a line through the maze from the arrow (➡) to the star (★).

■ Draw a line through the maze from the arrow (→) to the star (★).

Cristo Redentor on Corcovado's Hill

Brazil

■ Draw a line through the maze from the arrow (➡) to the star (★).

■ Draw a line through the maze from the arrow (➡) to the star (★).

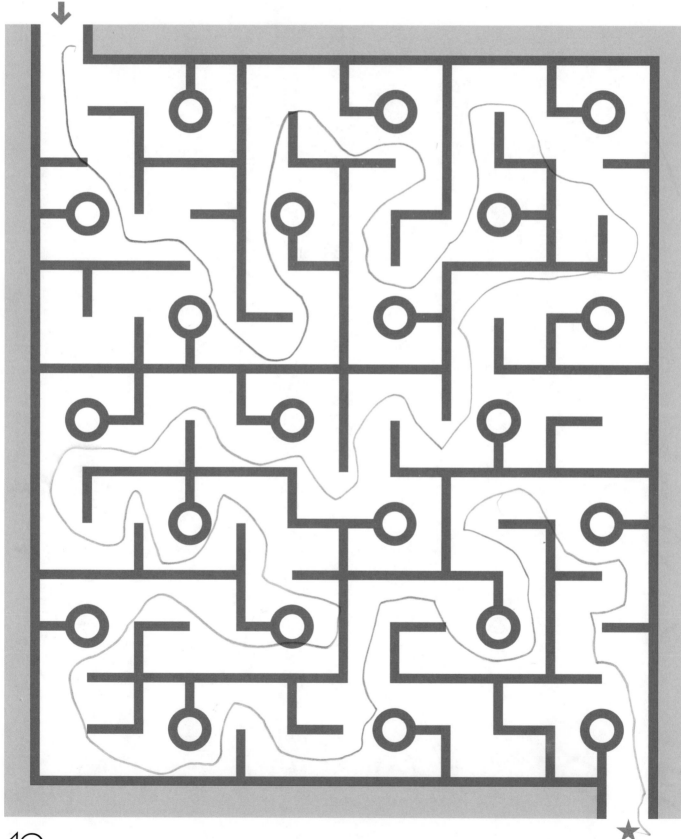

Mont-Saint-Michel

France

Name: Harry

Date: 4/30/15

■ Draw a line through the maze from the arrow (➡) to the star (★).

11

■ Draw a line through the maze from the arrow (→) to the star (★).

Great Buddha of Nara

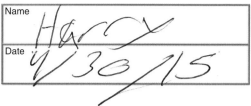

■ Draw a line through the maze from the arrow (→) to the star (★).

13

■ Draw a line through the maze from the arrow (➡) to the star (★).

Ayers Rock

Name Harry

Date 7/30/15

■ Draw a line through the maze from the arrow (➡) to the star (★).

15

■ Draw a line through the maze from the arrow (→) to the star (★).

16

Tower Bridge

United Kingdom

■ Draw a line through the maze from the arrow (➡) to the star (★).

■ Draw a line through the maze from the arrow (➡) to the star (★).

 # Mount Kilimanjaro

Kenya

Name Harry

Date 4/30/18

■ Draw a line through the maze from the arrow (➡) to the star (★).

■ Draw a line through the maze from the arrow (→) to the star (★).

Big Ben

United Kingdom

Name

Date

■ Draw a line through the maze from the arrow (➡) to the star (★).

21

■ Draw a line through the maze from the arrow (→) to the star (★).

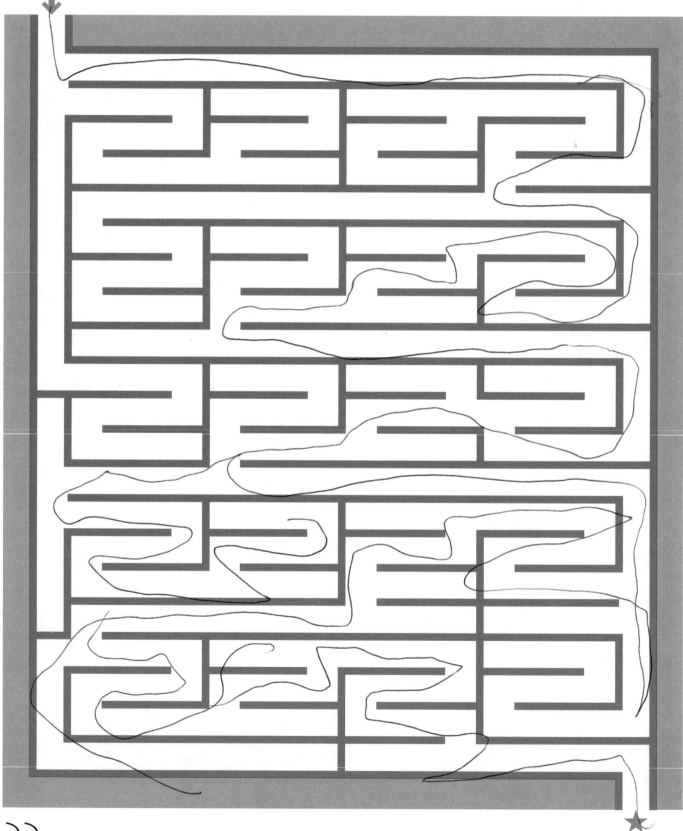

Michelangelo's Pieta

Name Harry

Date 4/30/15

■ Draw a line through the maze from the arrow (➡) to the star (★).

23

■ Draw a line through the maze from the arrow (➡) to the star (★).

Pyramid and Great Sphinx of Giza

Egypt

■ Draw a line through the maze from the arrow (➡) to the star (★).

26

Matterhorn

Switzerland

■ Draw a line through the maze from the arrow (➡) to the star (★).

27

■ Draw a line through the maze from the arrow (➡) to the star (★).

28

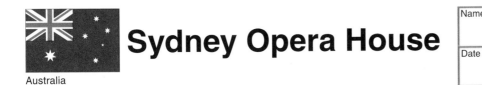

Sydney Opera House

Australia

Name
Date

■ Draw a line through the maze from the arrow (➡) to the star (★).

29

■ Draw a line through the maze from the arrow (➡) to the star (★).

France

Arc de Triomphe

■ Draw a line through the maze from the arrow (➡) to the star (★).

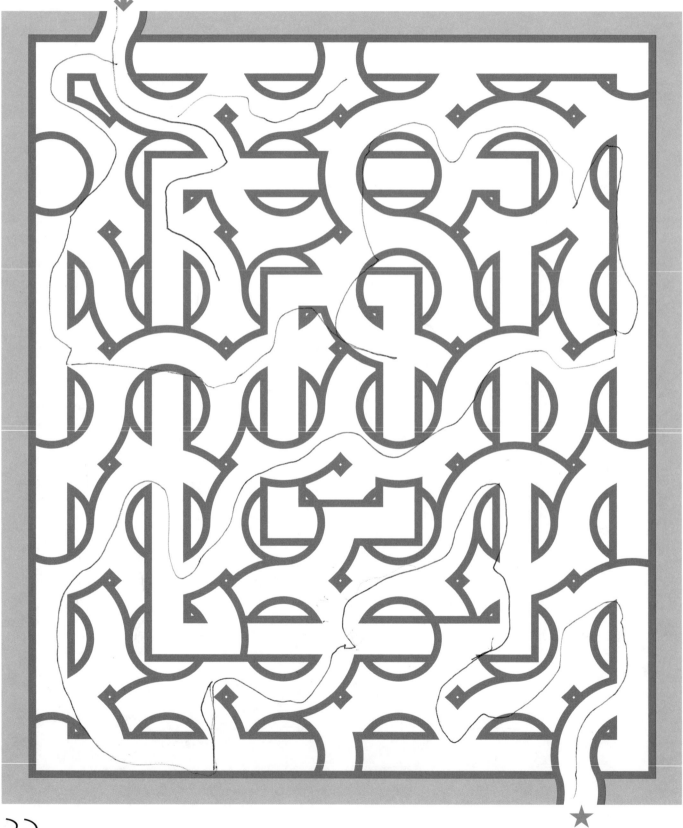

32

■ Draw a line through the maze from the arrow (➡) to the star (★).

■ Draw a line through the maze from the arrow (→) to the star (★).

![United States of America flag]

Manhattan

United States of America

To parents
In mazes like this one, the colored parts of the illustration are obstacles. Please help your child understand that he or she cannot find an exit path through any illustration that is in color.

Name

Date

■ Draw a line through the maze from the arrow (➡) to the star (★).

■ Draw a line through the maze from the arrow (→) to the star (★).

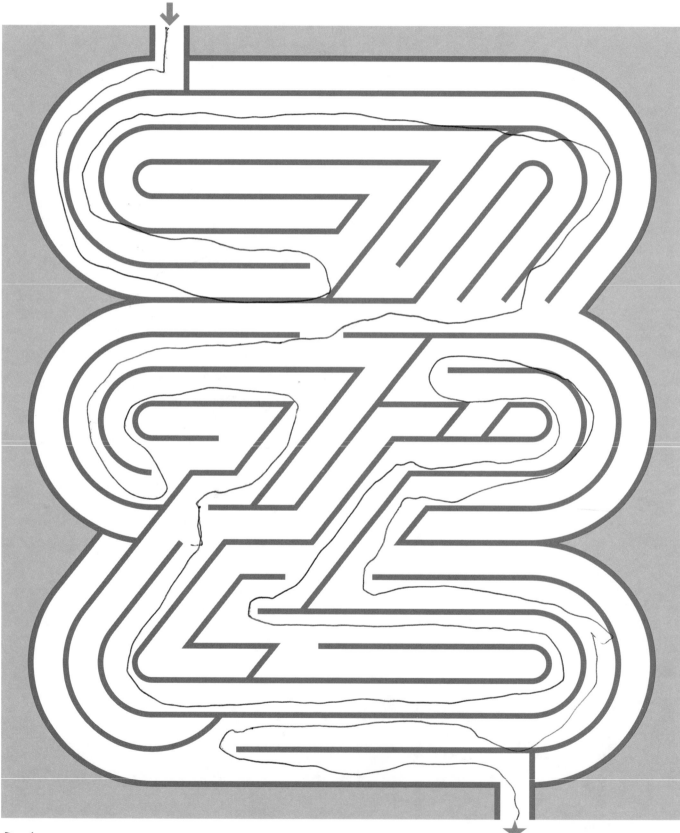

36

Pyramid at Chichen Itza

Name Henry

Date 5/1/ 36 BC

■ Draw a line through the maze from the arrow (➡) to the star (★).

■ Draw a line through the maze from the arrow (→) to the star (★).

38

Terracotta Warriors and Horses

China

■ Draw a line through the maze from the arrow (➡) to the star (★).

39

■ Draw a line through the maze from the arrow (➡) to the star (★).

Golden Gate Bridge

Name Skill X7Mz

Date 5/1/15

■ Draw a line through the maze from the arrow (➡) to the star (★).

41

■ Draw a line through the maze from the arrow (➡) to the star (★).

Machu Picchu

Name

Date

■ Draw a line through the maze from the arrow (➡) to the star (★).

43

■ Draw a line through the maze from the arrow (➡) to the star (★).

44

Forbidden City

Name

Date

■ Draw a line through the maze from the arrow (➡) to the star (★).

■ Draw a line through the maze from the arrow (→) to the star (★).

Niagara Falls

■ Draw a line through the maze from the arrow (➡) to the star (★).

■ Draw a line through the maze from the arrow (→) to the star (★).

Greece

Parthenon

Name

Date

■ Draw a line through the maze from the arrow (➡) to the star (★).

49

■ Draw a line through the maze from the arrow (→) to the star (★).

Windmill

Name

Date

■ Draw a line through the maze from the arrow (➡) to the star (★).

■ Draw a line through the maze from the arrow (→) to the star (★).

Great Wall of China

China

To parents

As your child progresses through this book, every maze is slightly harder than the last. If your child encounters difficulty, try giving him or her a hint.

Name

Date

■ Draw a line through the maze from the arrow (➡) to the star (★).

53

■ Draw a line through the maze from the arrow (→) to the star (★).

La Sagrada Familia

Name

Date

■ Draw a line through the maze from the arrow (➡) to the star (★).

■ Draw a line through the maze from the arrow () to the star (★).

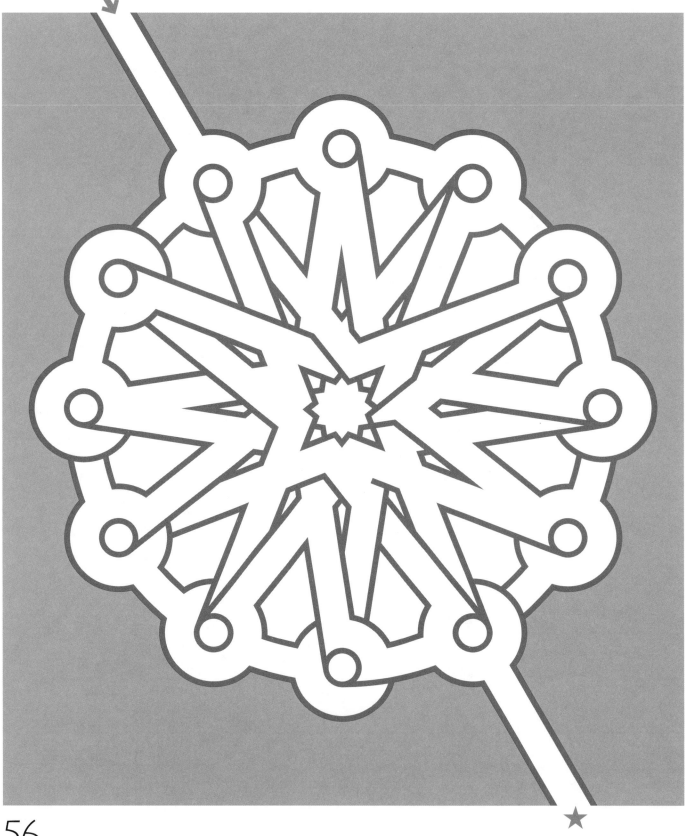

France

Basilica of the Sacre Coeur

■ Draw a line through the maze from the arrow (➡) to the star (★).

■ Draw a line through the maze from the arrow (➡) to the star (★).

Angkor Thom

Cambodia

Name

Date

■ Draw a line through the maze from the arrow (➡) to the star (★).

59

■ Draw a line through the maze from the arrow (→) to the star (★).

Japan

Himeji Castle

Name

Date

■ Draw a line through the maze from the arrow (➡) to the star (★).

■ Draw a line through the maze from the arrow () to the star (★).

Temple of the Dawn

Name

Date

■ Draw a line through the maze from the arrow (➡) to the star (★).

■ Draw a line through the maze from the arrow (➡) to the star (★).

India

Taj Mahal

■ Draw a line through the maze from the arrow (➡) to the star (★).

■ Draw a line through the maze from the arrow (➡) to the star (★).

Leaning Tower of Pisa

■ Draw a line through the maze from the arrow (→) to the star (★).

■ Draw a line through the maze from the arrow (➡) to the star (★).

68

Mosque of
Muhammad Ali

Egypt

Name

Date

■ Draw a line through the maze from the arrow (➡) to the star (★).

69

■ Draw a line through the maze from the arrow (➡) to the star (★).

Ponte di Rialto

Name

Date

■ Draw a line through the maze from the arrow (→) to the star (★).

■ Draw a line through the maze from the arrow (➡) to the star (★).

72

Blue Mosque

Turkey

■ Draw a line through the maze from the arrow (➡) to the star (★).

■ Draw a line through the maze from the arrow (→) to the star (★).

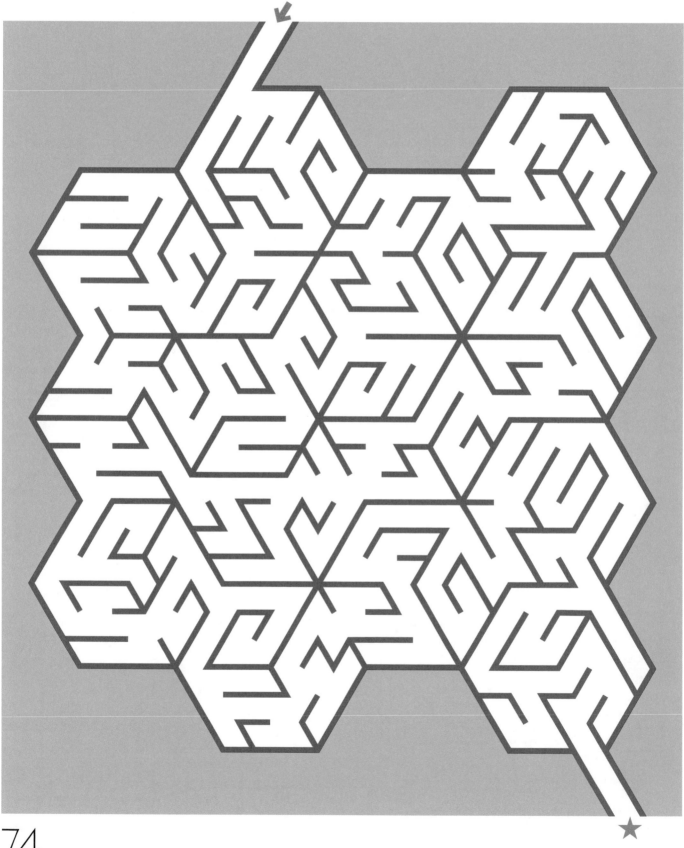

The Duomo of Florence

Italy

Name

Date

■ Draw a line through the maze from the arrow (➡) to the star (★).

75

■ Draw a line through the maze from the arrow (→) to the star (★).

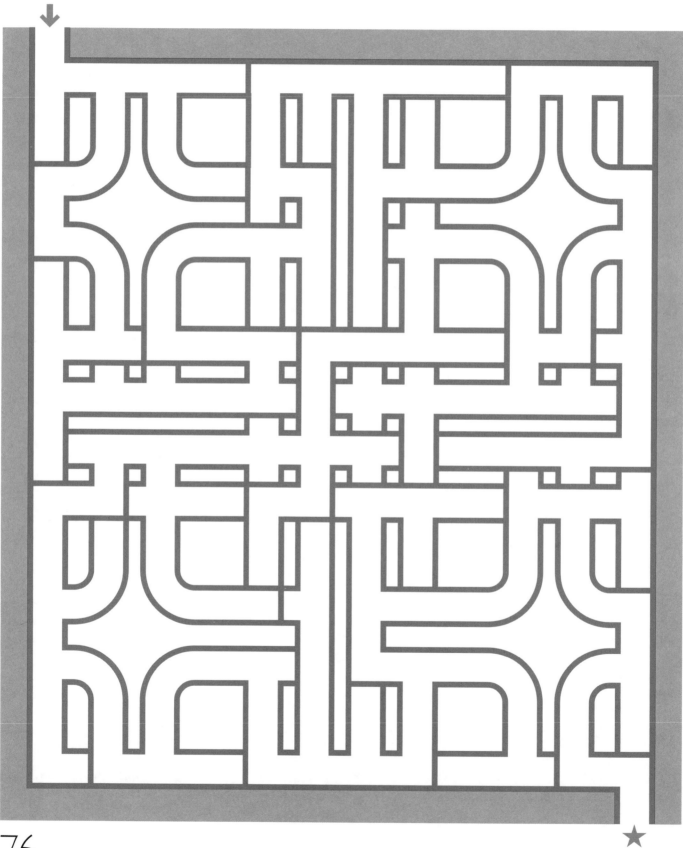

East Tower in Yakushi-ji Temple

Japan

■ Draw a line through the maze from the arrow (➡) to the star (★).

■ Draw a line through the maze from the arrow (➡) to the star (★).

Saint Basil's Cathedral in Red Square

■ Draw a line through the maze from the arrow (➡) to the star (★).

■ Draw a line through the maze from the arrow (➡) to the star (★).

KUM⊙N

Certificate of Achievement

is hereby congratulated on completing

My Book of Mazes: Around the World

Presented on _____, 2015

_____
Parent or Guardian

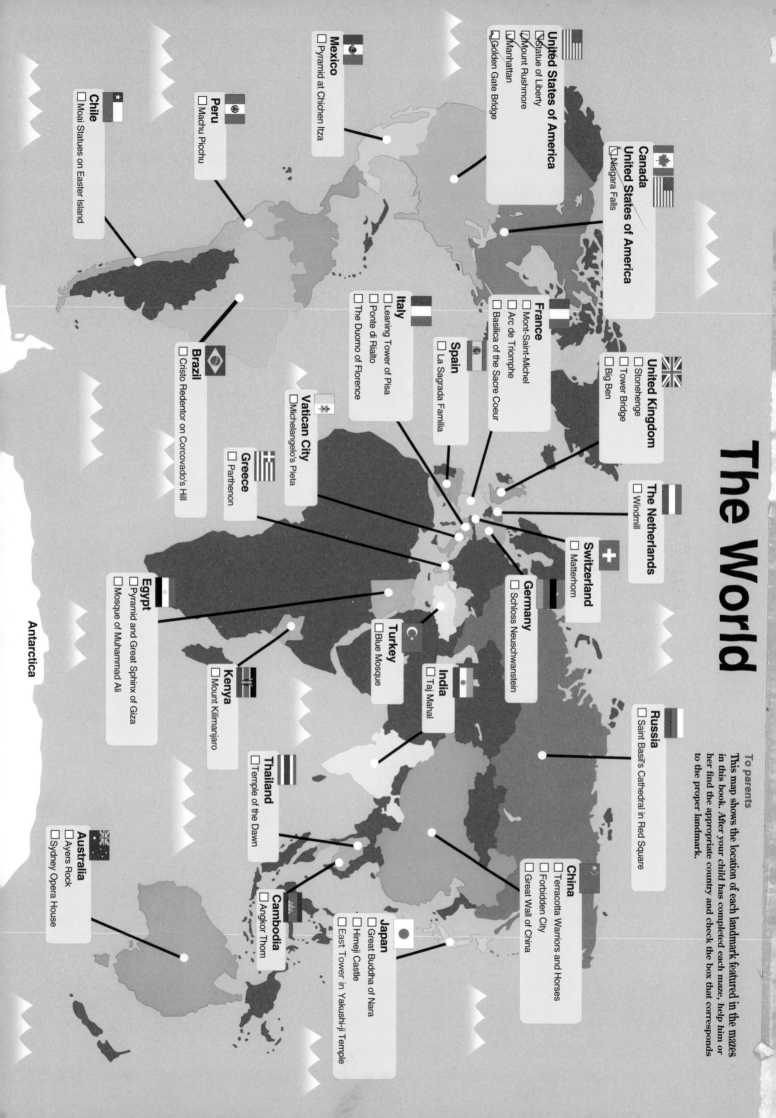

The World

To parents

This map shows the location of each landmark featured in the mazes in this book. After your child has completed each maze, help him or her find the appropriate country and check the box that corresponds to the proper landmark.

Canada
☐ Niagara Falls

United States of America

United States of America
☐ Statue of Liberty
☐ Mount Rushmore
☐ Manhattan
☐ Golden Gate Bridge

Mexico
☐ Pyramid at Chichen Itza

Chile
☐ Moai Statues on Easter Island

Peru
☐ Machu Picchu

Brazil
☐ Cristo Redentor on Corcovado's Hill

France
☐ Mont-Saint-Michel
☐ Arc de Triomphe
☐ Basilica of the Sacre Coeur

United Kingdom
☐ Stonehenge
☐ Tower Bridge
☐ Big Ben

Spain
☐ La Sagrada Familia

Italy
☐ Leaning Tower of Pisa
☐ Ponte di Rialto
☐ The Duomo of Florence

Vatican City
☐ Michelangelo's Pieta

Greece
☐ Parthenon

The Netherlands
☐ Windmill

Switzerland
☐ Matterhorn

Germany
☐ Schloss Neuschwanstein

Russia
☐ Saint Basil's Cathedral in Red Square

Egypt
☐ Mosque of Muhammad Ali
☐ Pyramid and Great Sphinx of Giza

Kenya
☐ Mount Kilimanjaro

Turkey
☐ Blue Mosque

India
☐ Taj Mahal

Thailand
☐ Temple of the Dawn

Cambodia
☐ Angkor Thom

China
☐ Terracotta Warriors and Horses
☐ Forbidden City
☐ Great Wall of China

Japan
☐ Great Buddha of Nara
☐ Himeji Castle
☐ East Tower in Yakushi-ji Temple

Australia
☐ Ayers Rock
☐ Sydney Opera House

Antarctica